# THE BATTLE
## OF THE
# LITTLE BIGHORN

By Mark Henckel

Illustrated by John Potter

## Dedication

*This book is dedicated to the warriors of both
nations who fought in this battle and to their
descendants in the hope of bringing about
understanding and growth for all.*

## Acknowledgments

We'd like to thank the following people for their generous assistance in the
gathering of research and checking of facts to make this book as historically
accurate as possible. Many thanks go to Superintendent Barbara Booher and the
staff of the Little Bighorn Battlefield National Monument, with special thanks to
Doug McChristian for his time and energy in providing reference material on the
Seventh Cavalry and aspects of the battle itself. Special thanks, too, to Mardell
Plainfeather, Kitty Belle Deernose, and LeAnn Simpson. Thanks also go to Diane
Svee, Margit Thorndal, Janet Southworth, and John Rogers for making sure the
material fits the educational needs of today's youth. And last, but surely not least,
warmest thanks to our wives, Cheryl and Carol, who endure not only the spread
of work throughout our houses, but suffer the emotional and financial
uncertainties of living with spouses with occupations like ours.

Falcon Press publishes and distributes a wide variety of books and
calendars, including children's books. You can get a free catalog by
writing Falcon Press, P.O. Box 1718, Helena, MT 59624, or calling
toll-free 1-800-582-2665. You can also get announcements of future
books in the Highlights from American History series, as well as
additional copies of this book.

Design, editing, typesetting, and other prepress work by Falcon Press,
Helena, Montana. Printed in Singapore.

Library of Congress Number 91-71544
ISBN 1-56044-042-2

# A Turning Point in History

On a hot summer day in 1876, hundreds of U.S. Army soldiers and Indian warriors spurred their horses into a battle that would become a legend—the Battle of the Little Bighorn.

In those days, the West rang with the clash of many battles between Indians and soldiers. But this battle, fought along the Little Bighorn River in what is now southeastern Montana, would stand out in history. It would capture the imagination of people for generations to come.

Why was this battle so special? Much of the reason is the mystery that surrounds it. The 210 soldiers led by Lieutenant Colonel George Armstrong Custer were completely wiped out by their Sioux and Northern Cheyenne foes. Not one lived to tell what happened.

This battle also marked a turning point in American history. It was the most horrible defeat ever suffered by the U.S. Army at the hands of the Plains Indians. And it signaled the end of the Sioux and Northern Cheyenne's free life on the plains. Never again would they score such a victory. From that time on, the U.S. government wouldn't rest until it forced the two tribes onto reservations.

The Battle of the Little Bighorn marked the end of an era and the start of a new one in the West.

# The Soldiers of the Seventh

The story begins on May 17, 1876. That day, General Alfred Terry led a force of infantry, cavalry, artillery, and mule-drawn wagons out of Fort Abraham Lincoln, which was built near where Bismarck, North Dakota, is today. There were about 925 men in all, including 600 cavalrymen. They planned to march halfway across Montana Territory to find the Sioux Indians. Then they intended to make the Sioux go to their reservation in Dakota Territory in what is now the western half of South Dakota.

Custer, who was 36 years old at the time, commanded the Seventh Cavalry as part of Terry's army. Some of his men were recent immigrants, especially Irish and Germans who had just come to the United States.

The average cavalryman was in his mid-twenties and unmarried. He had a horse and saddle, a bedroll, a few clothes, and some personal things such as a razor, comb, toothbrush, and mirror. A few might have had some paper and something to write with in their saddlebags, too. But many soldiers at the time couldn't read or write.

Unlike soldiers of today, who wear uniforms that are all pretty much alike, Custer's men dressed in a variety of clothes. They wore old uniform shirts and caps, straw hats, and buckskin

clothes. Most wore the standard sky-blue pants of the cavalry. They may have had nice new uniforms back at the fort, but there was no point in wearing them on a march like this one. After several months in the sweat and dust and mud, the men's clothes would get so dirty and smelly that it would be difficult to clean them. After long marches, many men just burned their clothes.

If it sounds like the soldiers didn't have much, they didn't. But for most of them, life was better than before they enlisted in the Army. They had clothes. They had warm blankets. They got three meals everyday. And they even earned a salary of thirteen dollars a month—more money than many of them had ever earned.

# The Man in Command

The man who led the Seventh Cavalry was George Armstrong Custer. He was considered a hero by many people in those days. He had temporarily been a general in charge of volunteers during the Civil War, but when the war was over he went back to a lower rank. In the years since the Civil War, he had explored and hunted in the West. Some people thought he was a great Indian fighter. They even thought he might make a good politician.

Custer's men still called him general, and a lot of people think he still thought of himself as one, too. He liked to give orders but not necessarily to take them. And if there was any action to be found, he wanted to be part of it. People who liked him said he was fearless and daring. Those who didn't like him thought he was impetuous and foolhardy.

The march with General Terry wasn't the first time Custer had traveled west from Fort Lincoln. In 1873, he had led a group of cavalrymen to protect survey crews that were looking for routes for the Northern Pacific Railway. A year later, he had led an Army force into the Black Hills of South Dakota. The expedition was supposed to explore the area, which was part of the Sioux reservation, and look for a site for a fort. But the men also were looking for the gold that was rumored to be in the Black Hills.

They found it, and their discovery helped to fuel the bad feelings the Sioux had for the white man. In the two years between the Black Hills Expedition and the Battle of the Little Bighorn, settlers and miners moved onto land in the Black Hills that had been given to the Sioux as part of their reservation.

The Sioux reservation was created in 1868 by the Fort Laramie Treaty. The treaty also gave the Sioux everything from the western boundary of their reservation to the Big Horn Mountains in Montana Territory as their hunting grounds. According to the treaty, they could go there to look for buffalo whenever they wanted.

Some government agents back on the reservation were crooked. They would take some of the beef and blankets that were supposed to be for the Sioux and sell them to other whites. The Indians on the reservation got what was left, and often it was rotten. The Indians sometimes starved. They began to wonder why they should stay on the reservation and eat beef that was crawling with worms when they could get fresh meat in Montana.

# A Way of Life Disappearing

By the summer of 1876, many Sioux were in Montana Territory. They were angry about the white men moving into the Black Hills and about the poor treatment the Indians received on the reservation. Some had never approved of the Fort Laramie Treaty, and they refused to live on the reservation.

Life for the Sioux in the mid-1870s was not as good as it had been before the white men came to the Great Plains—even for the Indians who didn't live on the reservation. As railroads and white settlers pushed west, the big herds of buffalo began to disappear. And the Sioux depended upon the buffalo for almost everything they needed. They made tipis from the animals' hides. They made spoons of their horns. They ate fresh buffalo meat in the summer and dried meat in the winter. Although they hunted for other

animals, such as deer, antelope, and elk, they considered the buffalo a vital part of their way of life.

So it's not surprising that the Sioux and their allies, the Northern Cheyenne, were out on their hunting grounds in the summer of 1876. When the deadline passed, most of the Indians who had never lived on the reservation had not shown up. Others who were on the reservation left to go hunting in the spring. So the government ordered the Army to get them back.

Custer knew how bad life was on the Sioux reservation. He had told officials in Washington, D.C., that the Indians were suffering, that the government agents were crooked, and that if he were a Sioux, he wouldn't stay on the reservation, either. But he was a soldier, and when he was ordered to do so, he still took part in the government's three-pronged attack on the Sioux.

# The Lay of the Land

The plan was for General Terry's army to head west from Fort Lincoln. Colonel John Gibbon would lead his troops eastward from Fort Ellis, at Bozeman, Montana Territory. And General George Crook would come north from Fort Fetterman in Wyoming Territory. The generals thought that at least one of the armies would find the Sioux.

But the country the three armies crossed was huge. The going was slow. Imagine what it must have been like for a foot soldier to walk halfway across North Dakota and almost halfway across Montana—a journey of hundreds of miles. And the armies had no short-wave radios or other ways to communicate with each other.

It took General Terry until June 8 to reach the junction of Rosebud Creek and the Yellowstone River. For two weeks, companies of soldiers explored the area, looking for the Indians and each other. Crook was nowhere to be seen. He had been defeated by the Sioux June 17 at the other end of Rosebud Creek and had turned back to Fort Fetterman. But Terry and Gibbon had no way of knowing.

As Crook found out, a lot more Sioux were off the reservation than the Army had thought. The government agents had lied about how many Sioux had left the reservation because they were afraid they would be sent less food and other rations. And all the Sioux seemed to be headed for their western hunting grounds.

By June, many of them had traveled through the Powder and Tongue river valleys of Montana Territory. This was one of their favorite places to hunt in the summer. There was plenty of game on the pine-covered ridges, in the big grassy valleys, and on the sagebrush-dotted slopes.

Even without the hunting, this was a busy time of year for the Indians. Each June they held their Sun Dance ceremony, the single most important event in their spiritual lives. The Sun Dance was a time when they honored their mother earth with prayers, singing, dancing, and fasting. It also was a time of great visions. And in June the Sioux and Northern Cheyennes usually got together with other members of their tribes after spending the winter apart in smaller villages or on the reservation at the various Indian agencies.

Many Indians gathered on the hills above Rosebud Creek for the Sun Dance that year, including the famous leaders Sitting Bull and Crazy Horse. No one knows exactly how many Indians were in the area in the weeks before the Battle of the Little Bighorn. But the size of the Sun Dance lodge and the remains of villages showed that it must have been a huge gathering.

As Terry marched up the Yellowstone River, scouts reported signs of big Indian movements in the area. On June 22, Custer was ordered to march south along Rosebud Creek, cut west to the Little Bighorn, and then march back north to rejoin Terry and Gibbon, who would come south up the Bighorn River. If the plan went well, the Indians would be caught in the middle.

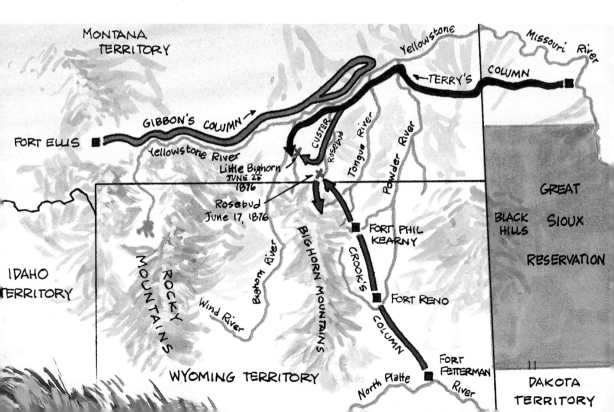

In the past, when the Army tried to catch up with the Indians of the plains, the Indians often saw the soldiers coming and seemed to vanish on the prairie. For that reason, Custer decided to travel light and quickly. He didn't take any cannons or fast-shooting Gatling guns with him. He took only his cavalry and pack mules as he looked for the Indian village. His force included thirty-one officers, 566 enlisted men, thirty-five Indian scouts, and about a dozen packers, guides, and civilians.

As Custer moved up the Rosebud on June 22, 23, and 24, he could see that the Indians had been in the area. He saw the trails left by the poles of the travois that the Indians used to carry their tipis and other belongings. He saw the hoofprints of their ponies. As he followed their trail past the Sun Dance site, he could tell that many Indians were on the move.

According to the false reports of the government agents back on the reservation, only about 800 warriors were out in the hunting territory. So Custer was confused when he came across so many camp sites along the Rosebud. He thought the Indians must not be moving very far between stops. But what he really was seeing was different camp rings from the same large group of Indians.

# A Village of Thousands

By this time, the Indians had moved over to the Little Bighorn River and set up their village. And what a village it was! Historians estimate that it held 7,500 to 8,000 Indians, including Sioux, Northern Cheyennes, and a few Arapahos. Among them were probably about 2,000 warriors.

There were six circles of tipis. Five of the circles held the lodges of the various bands of Sioux: the Hunkpapas, Oglalas, Miniconjous, Sans Arcs, Blackfoots, Two Kettles, Brules, and a few Yanktonais and Santees. The sixth circle held the Northern Cheyennes. The tipis stretched along the western bank of the Little Bighorn for almost three miles.

In the 1800s, most whites thought of Indians as unorganized savages. But each of the bands was well-organized for life on the prairie. Different warrior societies within the bands regulated the daily life of each circle. One society might be in charge of scouting. Another might be in charge of policing the members. Another might be in charge of defense. Still another might be out hunting to keep the band supplied with fresh meat.

Each tipi held one or two families, and each family member also had well-organized tasks. The father protected the family and provided it with meat. The mother took care of the lodge and kept the family clothed and fed. The youngest boys tended the family's horses. Older boys learned from the warriors and did chores for them. Girls helped their mothers cook, dry meat, dig roots, and pick berries. When everyone performed his chosen tasks successfully, the family prospered.

A warrior was considered wealthy if he had a lot of horses. Some had as many as 100. Some horses were used for hunting. Others were for packing. Still others were for racing. And some were for war. A village the size of the one on the Little Bighorn had a giant horse herd—maybe as many as 20,000 to 30,000 animals. They grazed near the village on the hills west of the river.

The village on the banks of the Little Bighorn may have been the biggest Indian gathering ever on the prairies. But there were reasons it was so big. For one thing, all the bands of Sioux had gathered as usual for the Sun Dance. For another, the Indians knew that the Army was looking for them. So they got together for protection. They may also have been celebrating their victory over General Crook. And a large herd of antelope spotted in the area kept them nearby to hunt for meat.

Finally, they stayed because of a vision that Sitting Bull had had during the Sun Dance. In the vision, Sitting Bull had seen soldiers falling upside-down into an Indian camp. The Sioux thought this meant that Sitting Bull and his people would win a great victory in the future and that many soldiers would die. With the strength of the vision to protect them, the Indians decided to stay for awhile on the banks of the Little Bighorn.

# A Fatal Decision

This was the scene that waited for Custer as he followed the Indian trail up Rosebud Creek. By the night of June 24, the trail had led him away from the creek and up toward the dividing ridge between the Rosebud and the Little Bighorn. The trail was fresh, and Custer thought he was getting close to the Sioux camp. He and his men continued up Davis Creek after dark. They stopped in the early hours of the morning to make their last camp.

Earlier in the night, Custer's Crow Indian scouts had climbed to a high hill called the Crow's Nest. At dawn on June 25, they could look down into the valley of the Little Bighorn. They couldn't see the Indian village, which was about fifteen miles away. But they could see signs that it was there. There was smoke in the distance. And they could see movement on the hills across the river that they knew must be the big horse herd.

Lieutenant Charles Varnum, who went with the Crows to scout the situation, couldn't see what the Indians did. The Crows told him to look for worms in the grass, the movement of something on the far slopes. He still couldn't see it. At mid-morning, Custer came to look. He couldn't see anything either, even though he used binoculars.

But the Crow scouts had seen enough. They told Custer that the village was a big one—too big for his force of cavalry. Civilian scouts Charley Reynolds and Mitch Bouyer knew it was too big, too. They believed that the cavalry would be doomed if it attacked. Some Arikara Indian scouts were so sure of the outcome of the battle ahead that they began singing their death songs. When Custer still made the decision to go on, one of his Indian scouts told him, "Today, you and I are going home on a path we do not know."

Despite the advice of the scouts, Custer thought he had a chance to attack the Indians before they could run and hide. In the past, Custer's attacks had often been reckless. But somehow, he had pulled them off without getting hurt. People called it Custer's luck. Maybe he thought he would be lucky again that June day. Maybe he thought of the glory he would have if he won a big victory over the Sioux. Maybe he thought his Seventh Cavalry was so good that it could beat any number of Indians. Maybe he just made a bad decision.

Custer told his officers he wanted to stay there between the Rosebud and Little Bighorn all day June 25. He wanted to begin his attack at dawn the next morning, when his men and their horses were well rested. That way, Custer could have surprised the Indians while they were still asleep in their lodges. But some things happened June 25 that made Custer think the Indians knew he was there.

For one thing, a box of hardtack bread had fallen off one of the pack mules back along the trail. When the soldiers noticed it was missing, they went back for it. They saw several Indians around the box trying to get it open. When the cavalrymen approached, the Indians rode away. The soldiers also saw another group of Indians, maybe a hunting party, and they worried that the Indians had seen them. And Custer knew that scouts from the Indian village might have seen his troops coming.

Because he thought he had been discovered, Custer decided at about noon to split up his force and attack the village that day. Captain Frederick Benteen would take three companies—about 125 men—and swing to the southeast to look for Indians. Major Marcus Reno would take another three companies—about 140 men—and ride down what is today called Reno Creek. Custer would take five companies—225 men—and ride to the north. Finally, Captain Thomas McDougall and 125 men would stay back and guard the pack mules, which carried the food and extra ammunition.

Soon after the three groups set out in the early afternoon, the horsemen discovered a single tipi. It turned out to be a burial lodge for Old She Bear, a Sioux warrior who had died from wounds he got fighting General Crook the week before. Army scouts set the tipi on fire, even though the smoke could alert the Indian village that the Army was near.

# "A Good Day to Die"

While the Army was approaching, the village was going about its daily business. It was Sunday afternoon. It was sunny and very hot, and there wasn't much wind. Many of the warriors were probably still asleep, even though it was well past noon. There had been a dance the night before, and the Indians had probably stayed up late, visiting and exchanging stories.

Because of the heat, boys who weren't in charge of watching the horse herd were probably swimming in the Little Bighorn. Women and girls were cooking, drying meat, digging wild turnips, and looking for early-ripening berries. The elders of the tribe were probably sitting around and talking of old times.

Because of the heat, the smoke flaps at the tops of the tipis were open. The bottoms of the tipis were probably rolled up to let the heat escape. Some warriors were working on weapons. Others were doing other tasks of their warrior societies. But mostly, the village was quiet that afternoon. The Indians knew the U.S. Army was in the area. But they felt safe because there were so many of them in the village. Surely no one would attack a village as large as this one. They decided not to attack the Army in the hope it would leave them alone.

It was into this scene, at about three in the afternoon, that Reno's men and his Indian scouts rode. Following Custer's orders, Reno crossed the Little Bighorn River and got his men ready to attack the southern end of the village.

The Sioux didn't spot Reno and his men until they had formed a battle line on the valley floor. So, despite all the fears that Custer's force had been spotted, the Sioux were surprised.

As Reno's men began moving toward the Hunkpapa circle of lodges at the southern end of the village, there must have been a lot of confusion among the Indians. Warriors rushed for their weapons. Young boys ran for the warriors' horses. Women and children looked for places to hide.

The Indians didn't fight in an organized way like the U.S. Army. They had no overall plan. There were no commands passed from colonels to majors to captains to lieutenants to sergeants to corporals to privates. Each Indian pretty much decided for himself what he was going to do.

Because of that, some of the warriors must have rushed into battle immediately when they saw Reno's troops. Others may have run to their lodges to get ready, painting their bodies and faces and putting on their finest clothes. Some may even have chosen not to fight at all. They may have thought the day just wasn't right for them to take part in a war.

In the Indian way, the leaders were warriors who led by their urging, their example, and their reputations more than by any rank that was awarded to them. Sitting Bull was reported to be in the Hunkpapa village as Reno approached, urging the warriors to fight. Crazy Horse did the same, saying, "It's a good day to die. Help the helpless ones."

# Reno's Retreat

Sitting Bull was well past the age of being a strong warrior. He was between forty-two and forty-five years old. Life was hard for the Indians on the plains, and so they aged quickly. In fact, sixty-five was considered to be very, very old. Any Indian who lived to such an age was thought of very highly because he had lived through a lot. By the time of the Little Bighorn, Sitting Bull was more of a spiritual leader to his people than a war leader. But he did his best to make sure the Sioux village was protected from the soldiers.

As Reno's men came up the valley, they were met by more and more Sioux warriors. Reno was probably looking hard for Custer, who had promised his help. He ordered his men to dismount and fight on foot while some of the soldiers took the horses into the cottonwood trees near the river for protection. More and more Sioux kept entering the fight.

The charging Sioux horses kicked up dust clouds, and the smoke of the rifles added to the haze. Gunshots and the shrieks of the Indians only made the scene more confusing for Reno and his men. The Arikara scouts, who were on the left end of the battle line, fell back. Then the Sioux under war chiefs Gall and Crow King had a way to get around behind Reno's men. Other Sioux began to come down the other side of the Little Bighorn to Reno's right. Reno began looking for a way to escape before all his men were killed.

At first, Reno moved back to the cottonwood trees and brush along the river. But the Sioux rode into the woods on horseback or sneaked in on foot. They threatened to wipe out all of Reno's command.

Reno decided to retreat when an Arikara Indian named Bloody Knife, Custer's favorite Indian scout, was killed. Bloody Knife was on horseback next to Reno when a Sioux bullet struck him in the head. Reno was so upset that he ordered his men to mount their horses, then dismount, and then mount again for a retreat back across the river.

With Sioux on all sides, Reno's men made a mad dash back to the south to find a place to cross the Little Bighorn River. The only place they could reach was a poor one with steep banks. More men fell to the Sioux as the survivors scrambled to the top of what is now called Reno Hill. They would be trapped there for the next day and a half.

After Reno attacked the southern end of the village, Custer decided to take his men across the hills to the northern end and attack there. If his plan had worked, the Sioux would have been caught between the two forces. They would have been split and disorganized as they tried to attack both.

But everything about the Army's plan went wrong. Reno awakened the village to the threat of the cavalry. He was beaten back, and finally he retreated to high ground with some of his wounded men. About the time Reno's attack was done, Custer's men rode toward a wide-awake village bristling with warriors who were armed and ready to shift their attention almost entirely to Custer.

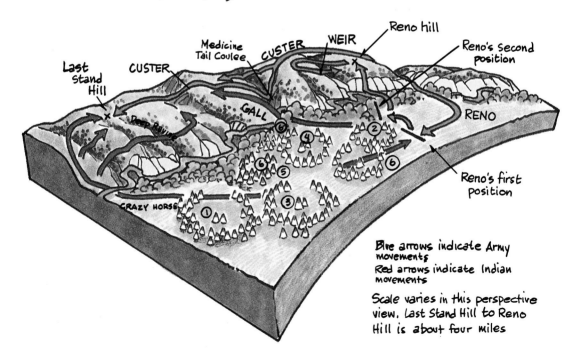

## BATTLE OF THE LITTLE BIGHORN

The Indian Village:
1. Northern Cheyenne Circle (120 Lodges)
2. Hunkpapa Sioux Circle (260 Lodges...)
3. Oglala Sioux Circle (240 Lodges)
4. Miniconjou Sioux Circle (150 Lodges)
5. Sans Arc Sioux Circle (110 Lodges)
6. Combined Blackfoot, Brule, and Two Kettle Sioux Circle (120 Lodges)

Blue arrows indicate Army movements
Red arrows indicate Indian movements

Scale varies in this perspective view. Last Stand Hill to Reno Hill is about four miles

# "Hurrah, Boys, We've Got Them!"

Custer thought he was going to score a major victory when he first saw the village. In fact, one of the last things anyone heard him say was, "Hurrah, boys, we've got them!" The remark was reported by trumpeter John Martin, an Italian immigrant whose real name was Giovanni Martini. He was the last man in the Seventh Cavalry to see Custer alive and live to tell about it.

One of Custer's officers, Lieutenant William Cooke, gave Martin a message to take back to Captain Benteen. It read, "Benteen. Come on. Big village. Be quick. Bring packs. W.W. Cooke."

Benteen read the message as he was coming back from his sweep to the south. He had found nothing there but dry, rugged hills. But before he could follow up on the order and go help Custer, he spotted Reno and his men on the hilltop. He decided instead to go to the aid of Reno, who might have been wiped out himself without Benteen's help.

No one really knows what happened to Custer and his men on that June day. No cavalrymen lived to tell about it. Indian accounts differed in many details. Dozens, if not hundreds, of possible battle plans have been drawn up in the years since to help guess what happened to Custer's command.

Most historians think Custer began his attack at about four in the afternoon. Part of his troops rode down Medicine Tail Coulee toward a shallow spot in the Little Bighorn River. From there, they could attack the village head-on. The rest of the soldiers rode north along what would become known as Battle Ridge.

We can only imagine Custer's charge toward the village. More than 200 horsemen kicked up the dust amid the crack of gunfire and the sounds of an army bugle. This was the kind of charge for which Custer had become famous. In the past, luck had always pulled him through. This time, Custer's luck ran out.

The soldiers were overwhelmed by the number of Sioux and Northern Cheyenne warriors riding out of the village. Just as the scouts had predicted, there were far too many Indians for the Seventh Cavalry to handle. For the soldiers, the battle was one long retreat back up the hills on the east side of the river.

The first warriors to lead the attack against Custer were Gall and Crow King. Gall's wife and children had been killed when Reno first attacked the village. Crazy Horse, Two Moons, and Lame White Man also charged in. They pushed the Army back up the hill and forced it to take defensive positions. Under the leadership of such officers as Lieutenant James Calhoun, Captain Tom Custer, Captain George Yates, Lieutenant Algernon Smith, and Captain Myles Keogh, the soldiers fought fiercely against the Indians. The warriors charged on their war ponies or crept on foot up the gullies toward the desperate soldiers.

# Custer's Last Stand

The situation was bad for the Seventh Cavalry. Curly, the only Crow scout who hadn't ridden with Reno, watched the death scene unfold before him. And he saw Sioux and Northern Cheyenne warriors gather a lifetime of glory for themselves in the Indian way.

According to the tribes' traditions, a warrior won honor in battle by "counting coup." A coup was an act of bravery, such as striking an enemy, stealing his weapon, or stealing his horse. If you were the first to strike an enemy, you counted a first coup, which was best of all. But there were also honors for the second and third coups.

It was important for a warrior to get a good start and build his reputation early in life. So Indian boys began their warrior duties early. At the age of twelve or thirteen, they went into battle with the warriors to hold their horses and to help them in other ways. By the time they were fourteen to sixteen, they were young warriors themselves.

These young warriors were among the Indians that swarmed up the hills after Custer's men. With rifles, clubs, spears, and bows and arrows, they rained fire on the troops. To the cavalrymen in the Seventh, the battle must have seemed like a nightmare. They had heard terrible stories about Indians and how fierce they were with their enemies. Some had witnessed this ferocity in earlier battles. They must have been incredibly afraid to see so many Sioux and Northern Cheyennes coming at them.

The Indians had their fears, too. Several chiefs had gone back East with the Army to visit government officials. They knew how many whites were back there. They knew those whites had cannons, Gatling guns, and rifles that could reach out and kill enemies from a long distance. But those fears were put aside on that Montana battlefield. The Indians had crushed Crook and repelled Reno. Now they were storming over Custer's men. It was only a matter of time before not a soldier would be left standing.

The Indians gradually pushed Custer's men back up the hill until the last men were holding out on top of what is now known as Last Stand Hill. A flanking blow was delivered by Crazy Horse, who had gone back to the village for a fresh war pony. While there, he was like a magnet, gathering warriors around him for a final charge up the north side of Last Stand Hill.

Near the end, a group of soldiers atop the hill huddled behind the dead bodies of their horses. The Northern Cheyennes and the

Sioux under Crazy Horse finally stormed over the top of this final position.

Some believe Custer was among the last men standing on Last Stand Hill. His body was found there. Others think he was killed earlier and his body was carried up the hill as the fight went on. It didn't really matter in the end. Custer and all of the men in his command were dead. His brothers Tom and Boston, his nephew Autie Reed, and his brother-in-law Calhoun were dead. Mark Kellogg, a newspaper correspondent for the *Bismarck Tribune* who rode a pack mule into the battle, had died. So had everyone else with Custer's command.

# The Disaster Is Discovered

Reno and his men had no way of knowing what was happening to Custer. They could hear gunshots in the distance. Some thought they should try to push through and help Custer. One of these was Captain Thomas Weir, who led a force of men to the north. He ran into so many Indians that he had to retreat back to Reno Hill.

The rest of that day and all of the next, Reno and Benteen and their men were pinned by Indians to the top of that hill. Indians shot at them from below. They threatened to creep up the hillside and attack. They probably could have rushed the hilltop at any time and killed all the soldiers the same way they wiped out Custer.

All that Reno and Benteen could do was wait and hope that Custer or Terry or Crook or someone would come to rescue them. The wounded men suffered in the heat. Their canteens were empty. The troopers held out as best they could. They scratched shallow holes in the hard Montana dirt so that they could hide from enemy bullets. They stacked up pack saddles and dead horses so that they could lie behind them.

During the long night of June 25, the men on the hill could hear some of the Indians celebrating. They also could hear the sad wailing of women who had lost husbands or sons in the battle. The next day, the men desperately fought back the charges of the warriors coming up the hill.

As dangerous as it was to move off the hill, the need for water for both the wounded and healthy men was getting worse as the morning wore on. Something had to be done. Some men volunteered to rush to the river with kettles and canteens to try to bring back water. They dashed downhill through a hail of bullets and arrows. They returned with only a little water, but it was enough to give the men some relief.

That afternoon, Reno and Benteen were surprised when the Indians started to retreat. Gradually, the warriors went away. By evening, the survivors of the Seventh Cavalry could see Indians moving up the valley. They were heading southwest, toward the Big Horn Mountains. They had set fire to the dry grass in the valley bottom. The smoke hid their movements, and the flames destroyed grass that otherwise might feed the Army's horses.

The men on Reno Hill spent a quiet but uneasy night worrying that the warriors might return. But at dawn, not an Indian was in sight. The troopers breathed a little easier.

At mid-morning on Tuesday, June 27, Reno's men saw dust kicked up by horses' hooves to the north. At first they thought it must be Custer. But it was Terry and Gibbon instead. And what these men had to report would send shock waves throughout the entire country.

On the ridge above the valley of the Little Bighorn, Gibbon's scouts had found that every man of Custer's command had been killed. The only Army survivor of the battle was said to be Keogh's horse, Comanche, which was badly wounded. Dead soldiers and dead and dying horses littered the battlefield.

In all, 210 men died with Custer. Another fifty-three of Reno's men died, and sixty more were wounded. No one knows exactly how many Sioux and Northern Cheyennes died. Estimates vary from thirty to 300.

# The Price of Change

The Battle of the Little Bighorn was the last big victory for the Sioux and Northern Cheyennes. It was the last big defeat on the plains for the U.S. Army.

In the days after the battle, the Indians headed toward the Big Horn Mountains. From there, they broke up into small groups. Many found their way back to the reservation in Dakota Territory.

Terry sent word of the battle back to the Army in Washington, D.C. Furious and horrified, the Army sent more soldiers to the West. They kept after the Sioux and Northern Cheyennes until the tribes' free life on the plains was gone forever.

People often look for good guys and bad guys in a conflict like the Battle of the Little Bighorn. Some might think that Custer and his men, in their greed for victory, were all bad—that Crazy Horse and the Sioux, in their defense of their village, were all good. But for the most part, Custer and his men were just soldiers following orders that were given to them by the U.S. government. And Crazy Horse and the other Indians were trying to protect a way of life that could not withstand the westward movement of the white people.

In the end, the real meaning of Custer's Last Stand can't be measured in terms of good guys and bad guys. It's just one part of a story of two very different peoples who had two very different ways of life. June 25, 1876, will always be remembered as a turning point for the Sioux and Northern Cheyenne people and for the Army of the West. And it will always hold a bit of mystery for anyone who takes the time to learn more about the fascinating Battle of the Little Bighorn.

G.A. CUSTER
BVT. MAJ. GEN.
LT. COL.

# Learn More About It

If you would like to learn more about the Battle of the Little Bighorn, visit the Little Bighorn Battlefield National Monument, about sixty miles southeast of Billings, Montana. A museum at the visitor center features many military and Indian artifacts, artwork, dioramas, and audio-visual programs.

You may also tour the battlefield. A 4.5-mile road runs from the hill where Reno and Benteen were pinned down to the site of Custer's Last Stand. On Last Stand Hill, white marble markers show where many of the troopers died. A granite monument, erected in 1881, bears the names of all the officers and soldiers killed in the battle. Their bodies were buried in a common grave around the base of the monument.

For more information about the battlefield, write Little Bighorn Battlefield National Monument, P.O. Box 39, Crow Agency, MT 59022. Or call (406) 638-2621.

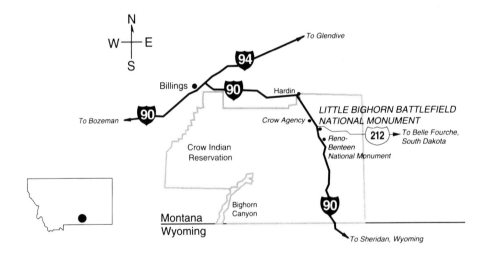